GW01018313

Michel Thomas

FRENCH LANGUAGE BUILDER

Hodder & Stoughton

A MEMBER OF THE HODDER HEADLINE GROUP

Press reviews for *Michel Thomas Language Courses*

The Times
'the nearest thing to painless learning'

The Daily Telegraph
'works like a dream'

Sunday Business
'…ideal for any business traveller who needs to be able to get around confidently'

Time Out
'…five minutes into the first CD, you already feel like you're winning'

Red
'Hugely inspiring'

Daily Star
'Michel's methods will teach you effectively and easily'

The Daily Telegraph
'a great way to learn; it's fast and it lasts'

First published in UK 2001 by Hodder Headline Ltd, 338 Euston Road, London NW1 3BH.

Copyright © 2001 Michel Thomas

Typeset by Transet Limited, Coventry, England.
Printed in Great Britain by Circle Services Ltd, Southend-on-Sea, Essex

Introduction

Who is Michel Thomas?

Michel Thomas is head of the Michel Thomas Language Centers and has been teaching languages for over fifty years, primarily in New York, Beverly Hills, and London. He is a graduate of the Department of Philology at the University of Bordeaux, France, and has studied psychology at the Sorbonne (Paris) and at the University of Vienna. However, it is his remarkable life experiences that have fuelled his passion for teaching languages*.

Michel spent most of his childhood in Germany and France. With the rise of Hitler, he began his years of escape and resistance. He spent two brutal years in French concentration and slave labour camps, constantly threatened by deportation to German death camps. He escaped and fought for the French Resistance, surviving capture, interrogation and torture.

Michel's wartime experiences, particularly his torture by the Gestapo when he discovered the ability to block out pain, made Michel Thomas aware of the untapped potential of the human mind. However, it was his deeply held conviction that the biggest weapon in maintaining a free society was education that drove him to devote his life to probing the learning process. Michel moved to Los Angeles in 1947, and he set up a language institute in Beverly Hills. Over a period of fifty years, he has developed a unique and revolutionary learning system that has made him the world's leading language teacher.

*For a full account of his fascinating life, read 'The Test of Courage: Michel Thomas' by Christopher Robbins, published by Random House

What is the Michel Thomas method?

Over a period of fifty years, Michel Thomas has developed and perfected a unique method of teaching languages**. In essence, he breaks a language down to its component parts and enables learners to reconstruct the language themselves to form their own sentences, to say what they want, when they want. The experience of learning a language becomes so exciting and satisfying that it stimulates self-motivation and builds confidence.

Who is the *French Language Builder* for?

People who have already learned French with Michel Thomas

The *Language Builder* does just what its name suggests: it builds on the language Michel teaches in his 8-hour course. It does this in two important and inseparable ways: by echoing the 8-hour course to review key structures, while at the same time presenting new idioms (which are heard and used all the time in everyday French but which are very rarely taught). This dual approach means that you painlessly review what you have learned as you simultaneously expand the range of your working and functional knowledge of the language.

People who have learned French using other methods

You may have learned French before and now want to brush it up for a holiday or business trip, or perhaps you are looking for a new approach to help with revision or to re-motivate you, either way, the *Language Builder* will give you a real insight into how the language works and will boost your confidence to speak.

You may find that it takes a while to get used to Michel's innovative way of teaching – it is certainly quite unlike any other method you will have come across – but once you have experienced the excitement of painless learning you will be hooked!

**U.S. patent pending. All rights reserved

What does the pack contain?

The pack comprises approximately two hours of recorded material plus a 48-page booklet. The recordings are available on CD or audio cassette and feature Michel Thomas alone. To avoid wasting recording time, there are no pauses on the recordings, but you are strongly recommended to use the pause button on your player for maximum learning (see below). The booklet contains the key words and phrases to help you with written French, but you do not need to use it at all if you just want to concentrate on improving your speaking and listening skills.

How do I use the recordings?

• Relax!

As far as possible, make yourself comfortable before playing the recordings and try to let go of the tensions and anxieties traditionally associated with all learning.

• Interact fully with the recordings

Use the pause button to stop the recording so that you have time to think out your translations. Then say the phrase or sentence out loud (or in a whisper, or in your head, if you are in a public place), before Michel does. This is essential. You do not learn by repetition but by thinking out the sentences yourself; it is by your own thought process that you truly learn.

• Stop the recording whenever it suits you

You will notice that the recordings are not divided into lessons*** so it is easy to stop wherever you want.

*** Tracking breaks have been inserted on the CDs: you may find it helpful to make a note of these (or the timings, if you have audio cassettes) in this booklet to help you get back immediately to where you left off or to review specific points

What level of language will I achieve?

The recordings will give you a practical and functional use of the spoken language. Michel Thomas teaches the everyday conversational language that will allow you to communicate in a wide variety of situations, empowered by the ability to create your own sentences and use the language naturally.

How can I go on to improve further?

Obviously, nothing compares with first-hand contact with native French speakers, but if this is not possible for you, Michel recommends reading French newspapers and magazines as one of the best ways to keep up and extend your language. Interviews are particularly good, as they reflect French as it is actually being spoken, rather than the language taught in schools or textbooks.

Who has Michel Thomas taught?

People travel from all over the world to learn a foreign language with Michel Thomas – because his method works. His students, now numbering in the thousands, have included well-known people from the arts and from the corporate, political and academic worlds. Michel's list of clients include:

• *Celebrities*: Mel Gibson, Emma Thompson, Woody Allen, Barbra Streisand, Warren Beatty, Melanie Griffith, Eddie Izzard, Bob Dylan, Jean Muir, Donald Sutherland, Jane Fonda, Anne Bancroft, Mel Brooks, Nastassja Kinski, Carl Reiner, Raquel Welch, Johnny Carson, Julie Andrews, Isabelle Adjani, Candice Bergen, Barbara Hershey, Priscilla Presley, Loretta Swit, Tony Curtis, Diana Ross, Herb Alpert, Angie Dickinson, Lucille Ball, Doris Day, Janet Leigh, Natalie Wood, Jayne Mansfield, Ann-Margaret, Yves Montand, Kim Novak, Otto Preminger, Max Von Sydow, Peter Sellers, François Truffaut, Fanny Ardant.

• *Diplomats, dignitaries and academics*: Former U.S. Ambassador to France, Walter Curley; U.S. Ambassador to the U.N., Joseph V. Reed; Cardinal John O'Connor, Archbishop of New York; Anthony Cardinal Bevilacqua, Archbishop of Philadelphia; Armand Hammer; Sarah Ferguson, Duchess of York; Professor Herbert Morris, Dean of Humanities at UCLA; Warren Keegan, Professor of Business at Pace University in New York; Professor Wesley Posvar, former President of the University of Pittsburgh.

• *Executives from the following corporations*: AT&T International, Coca-Cola, Proctor & Gamble, Chase Manhattan Bank, American Express, Merrill Lynch, New York Chamber of Commerce and Industry, Boeing Aircraft, General Electric, Westinghouse Electric, Bank of America, Max Factor, Rand Corporation, Bertlesmann Music Group-RCA, Veuve Cliquot Inc., McDonald's Corporation, Rover, British Aerospace.

What do his students say?

Academy® award winning director and actress, **Emma Thompson** (as quoted in the *Guardian*): 'The excitement of learning something new was overwhelming. Michel not only taught me Spanish, he opened my eyes to the possibilities of a completely different kind of learning. Michel forbids his students to practise, or to try to remember. Michel takes the burden off the student and upon himself… Learning Spanish with Michel was the most extraordinary learning experience of my life – it was unforgettable.'

New York film-maker **Woody Allen**, (as quoted in *USA Today* and *Business Life*): 'I am a poor student, particularly with languages. I had years of Spanish in school and could never speak a word... (but) learning with Michel: it's like a kid who loves baseball and who just knows every ball player, every batting average, every statistic about the game. They've learned it all effortlessly. It's the same with Michel. You learn a language effortlessly. It is amazing. (He)…had me speaking French and I learned it in a way I've never forgotten, and it was painless. A tremendous experience.'

Customer feedback

'I am writing to congratulate you on the highly original and successful language courses by Michel Thomas; I am currently working on German and French while my daughter, at my suggestion, has bought the Italian course.'

R Harris

'I have now finished the eight cassette Italian course and would like to say how pleased I am with it. I am a scientist, with all my neurones in the side of my brain that deals with understanding, and next to none on the side that deals with memory. This has meant my ability to retain vocabulary and learn a language has been about as bad as it comes. Against all odds, the Michel Thomas course has left me with a real sense of achievement, and a tremendous basis for further progress in learning Italian.'

T A Whittingham

Recording 1

Je veux… *I want*
Je le veux *I want it*
Je veux ça *I want that*
Je veux l'avoir *I want to have it*
Je veux avoir ça *I want to have that*

Je voudrais… *I would like…*
…le/la voir *…to see it/him/her*
…beaucoup la voir *…very much like to see her*

Je dois… *I must…*
…parler avec elle/lui *…speak with her/him*
…lui parler *…talk to him/her*

J'aime… *I like, I love…*
…le faire *…to do it*

Je voudrais y aller *I would like to go there*

You could say Je voudrais aller là *for 'I would like to go there', but it is much better to use* y
y *means 'to it' or 'there' and as a pronoun comes before the verb*
You can push the '-s' of je voudrais *into* y aller

Je vais y aller *I am going to go there*
J'y vais *I am going there*

quelquefois *sometimes*
une fois, deux fois, trois fois *once, twice, three times*
pour la première / dernière fois *for the first / last time*
pour la prochaine fois *for the next time*

J'y vais quelquefois	*I go there sometimes*
…mais pas souvent	*…but not often*
très souvent / pas très souvent	*very often / not very often*
…mais pas très souvent	*…but not very often*

C'est rare — *It's rare*

Ce n'est pas très intéressant — *It isn't very interesting*

> *You can push the 's' of* très *into* intéressant

d'ailleurs… — *besides…*

…je n'aime pas le faire — *…I don't like to do it*

C'est trop loin — *It is too far*

C'est très loin	*It is very far*
C'est très loin d'ici	*It is very far from here*
Et d'ailleurs, c'est trop loin d'ici	*And besides, it's too far from here*
C'est loin d'ici?	*Is it far from here? /*
	How far is it from here ?
Ce n'est pas loin	*It's not far*

C'est près — *It is near*

C'est près d'ici — *It is near here [near from here]*

Aller à pied — *to go on foot / to walk*

Vous pouvez aller à pied	*You can go on foot / walk*
C'est trop loin pour y aller à pied	*It is too far to walk there*

> *When 'to' in English means 'in order to' you use* pour *followed by the verb*

Vous pouvez prendre un taxi	*You can take a taxi*
On doit y aller en voiture	*One must go there by car [in car]*

You can push the 't' of doit *into* y aller

On peut / doit prendre un taxi pour y aller	*One can / must take a taxi to go there*

Ça va   *It's all right [it goes, it is going]*

C'est bien, Ça va bien	*It's fine, It's going fine*
Ça va bien comme ça	*It's all right that way / like that*
C'est mieux	*It's better*
Ça va mieux maintenant	*It's going better now*
Tout va mieux maintenant	*Everything is going better now*
Ça va beaucoup mieux comme ça	*It's going much better that way / like that*

Qu'est-ce que vous préférez?	*What do you prefer?*
Je le préfère comme ça	*I prefer it like that*
Je l'aime…	*I like it…*
…comme ça	*…that way*
…mieux comme ça	*…better that way*
…beaucoup mieux comme ça	*…much better that way*

Je n'aime pas y aller maintenant	*I don't like to go there now*

vraiment   *really*

Je ne l'aime pas vraiment	*I don't really like it*
Je n'aime pas vraiment y aller	
Vraiment je n'aime pas y aller	*I don't really like to go there*
pas vraiment	*not really*

vraiment *means 'really' or 'truly'*
vrai *means 'true';* c'est vrai *means 'it's true';* Ah vraiment? *means 'Is that so?'*

en tout cas…	*at any rate [in all case]…*
…pas ce soir	*…not tonight*
…parce que je suis trop fatigué(e)	*…because I am too tired*
Je préfère rester ici	*I prefer [to stay] staying here*
J'aime mieux rester ici	*I like better staying here*
Je n'ai pas envie de…	*I don't feel like…*
…sortir	*…going out*

avoir envie de *means 'to feel like something'*
A noun or an adjective needs de *if it is followed by a verb*

Je n'ai pas envie de…	*I don't feel like…*
…le faire	*…doing it*
…le voir	*…seeing it*
…rester ici	*…staying here*
Je n'ai pas envie d'…	*I don't feel like…*
…aller le voir	*…going to see it*
…y aller ce soir	*…going there tonight*
J'ai vraiment envie d'aller au cinéma ce soir	*I really feel like going to the movies tonight*
J'ai envie de voir ce film	*I feel like seeing this picture*
J'ai envie d'aller voir ce film	*I feel like going to see this picture*
Il paraît	*It appears, it seems*
Il paraît que c'est très intéressant	*It appears that it is very interesting*
Il paraît que c'est un film très intéressant	*It appears that it is a very interesting picture*
J'ai envie de le voir	*I feel like seeing it*

Ça m'intéresse	*It interests me*
Ça m'intéresse beaucoup	*It interests me very much*
Ça ne m'intéresse pas	*It doesn't interest me*

| **pas du tout** | *Not at all* |
| Ça ne m'intéresse pas du tout | *It doesn't interest me at all* |

Je le trouve…	*I find it, I think it is…*
…très intéressant	*…very interesting*
Qu'est-ce que vous pensez?	*What do you think?*
	[What is it that you think?]
Qu'est-ce que vous en pensez?	*What do you think of it?*

A mon avis…	*In my opinion…*
…on peut y aller	*…one/we can go there*
…nous pouvons y aller	*…we can go there*

On, meaning 'one', is very often used for 'we' instead of the nous *form*

Ça vaut la peine	*It is worth the trouble*
Ça vaut la peine de le faire	*It is worth doing it*
Ça ne vaut pas la peine de le faire	*It is not worth doing it*
Ça ne vaut pas la peine d'y aller	*It is not worth going there*

For 'It's not worth it' you can also say Ce n'est pas la peine

Je crois que…	*I think/believe that…*
…ça vaut la peine	*…it's worth it*
…ça vaut la peine d'y aller le voir	*…it's worth going there to see it*

peut-être	*perhaps*
Mais peut-être pas ce soir	*But perhaps not tonight*
Peut-être demain soir…	*Perhaps tomorrow night…*

11

| …si vous voulez | …if you like |
| …si vous avez envie de le faire | …if you feel like doing it |

You can push the 'z' of avez *into* envie

Ça me plaît
It appeals to me, it pleases me, I like it

Je voudrais l'avoir parce que ça me plaît	I would like to have it because I like it
Ça me plaît beaucoup	It pleases me very much
Ça vous plaît?	It pleases you? Do you like it?

plaît *as in* s'il vous plaît *meaning 'please', literally 'if it pleases you'*

Vous le voulez?	You want it?
Est-ce que vous le voulez?	Do you want it? [Is it that you want it?]
Vous voulez l'avoir?	You want to have it?

FORMING A QUESTION
The simplest way of forming a question is to say a statement in a questioning tone. Another easy way is to put Est-ce que… *[Is it that…] at the beginning of a statement.*

Vous en voulez?
You want some of it?

Vous voulez en avoir?	You want to have some of it?
Combien en voulez-vous?	How much of it do you want?
J'en veux	I want some
Je n'en veux pas	I don't want any
Je n'en veux plus	I don't want any more of it

en *means 'of it'; it is a pronoun and comes before the verb*

tant pis
too bad, so what

tant *means 'so much',* pis *means 'worse', literally 'so much the worse'*

tant mieux	*so much the better*
tant mieux pour moi	*so much the better for me*
tant pis pour vous	*so much the worse for you*
Combien c'est? C'est combien?	*How much is it?*
Combien ça vaut?	*How much is it worth?*
Ça ne vaut pas grand-chose	*It's not worth much [big thing]*
Ça me plaît beaucoup	*I like it very much*
Je dois l'avoir	*I must have it*
Combien je vous dois?	*How much do I owe you?*

Je dois means both 'I must' and 'I owe'

Ça ne me plaît pas	*I don't like it*
Ça vous plaît?	*Do you like it?*
Est-ce que ça vous plaît?	*Does it appeal to you, Do you like it?*
	[Is it that you like it?]
Ça ne me plaît pas de le faire	*I don't like doing it*
Je suis très content…	*I am very glad…*
…de vous voir	*…to see you*
Je suis très heureux…	*I am very happy…*
…de vous voir	*…to see you*
…de l'arranger pour vous	*…to arrange it for you*
heureusement	*fortunately, happily*
Heureusement ça sera possible de le faire	*Fortunately it will be possible to do it*

malheureusement — *unfortunately*

Mais malheureusement je ne peux pas le faire aujourd'hui — *But unfortunately I can't do it today*

Je ne peux pas le faire — *I cannot do it*

Je ne peux rien faire… — *I cannot do anything…*

…mais possiblement demain — *…but possibly tomorrow*

Si ça vous va — *If it is all right with you [if it goes to you]*

Il y a… — *There is, There are…*

Il y a beaucoup de monde — *There are many people*

> le monde *means 'world', as in* tout le monde *'everybody' (literally 'all the world')*

Tout le monde est là — *Everybody is there*

Il y a trop de monde — *There are too many people*

Il y a un message pour vous — *There is a message for you*

Il n'y a pas de messages — *There are no messages*

Est-ce qu'il y a des messages? — *Are there any messages?*

Rien aujourd'hui — *Nothing today*

Plus rien — *Nothing any more*

Il n'y a plus rien — *There is nothing any more*

Je voudrais laisser un message — *I would like to leave a message*

Est-ce que je peux laisser un message? — *Can I leave a message/ message?*

Je peux laisser un message?

> laisser *means 'to leave' or 'to leave behind'*

Je le cherche…	*I am looking for it*
…partout	*…everywhere*
Je le vois partout	*I see it everywhere*
Je le cherche partout mais…	*I'm looking for it everywhere but…*
…je ne peux pas le trouver	*…I cannot find it*

chercher *means 'to look for' or 'to search', as in* chercher la femme, *'to look for the woman'*

Je ne sais pas où c'est	*I don't know where it is*
Regardez! C'est là	*Look! It's there.*
C'est là-bas	*It's over there*

regarder *means 'to look';* chercher *means 'to look for'*

Moi, je sais où c'est	***I** know where it is*

Use moi *to emphasise 'I'. In English, for emphasis, we raise our voice instead*

Voulez-vous l'apporter?	*Will you bring it?*
Voulez-vous me l'apporter?	*Will you bring it to me?*
Je l'apporte	*I'm bringing it*
Je vous l'apporte	*I'm bringing it to you*

apporter *means 'to bring';* porter *means 'to carry' and also 'to wear'*

bien sûr	*of course*
naturellement	*naturally*

aller + chercher *means 'to get', so* je vais le chercher *doesn't mean 'I am going to look for it', but 'I am going to get it'. 'I will look for it' is* je le chercherai

Je sais où c'est et je vais le chercher	*I know where it is and I am going to get it*
Je dois me dépêcher	*I must hurry [I must dispatch myself]*
Je vais me dépêcher	*I am going to hurry*
Voulez-vous vous dépêcher?	*Will you hurry ?*
Je suis pressé	*I am in a hurry, I am pressed for time*
Je suis très pressé	*I am very much in a hurry*
Je dois me dépêcher parce que…	*I must hurry because*
…je suis très pressé	*…I am very pressed for time*
Il y a beaucoup de…	*There is a lot of…*
…circulation	*…traffic*
Il y a trop de…	*There is too much…*
…circulation	*…traffic*
Ça va prendre très longtemps…	*It is going to take a very long time…*
…pour y arriver	*…to get there*
en retard	*late*
Je vais être en retard	*I am going to be late*
Je serai là / J'y serai en retard	*I will be there late*
Je serai là dans quelques minutes	*I will be there in a few minutes*

In French there is a difference between 'late' meaning 'belated' as in Je suis en retard *and 'late' as in 'It is too late'* C'est trop tard

quelque chose	*something*
Est-ce qu'il y a quelque chose pour moi?	*Is there something for me?*
Non, il n'y a rien	*No, there isn't anything*
Qu'est-ce que vous avez pour moi?	*What do you have for me?*

quelque chose à… *something to…*

Est-ce que vous avez quelque chose *Do you have something to eat?*
   à manger?

J'ai quelque chose à vous dire *I have something to tell you*
J'ai beaucoup de choses à faire *I have many things to do*

Je n'ai rien à faire maintenant *I have nothing to do now*
Rien à faire *Nothing doing*

Ça ne fait rien *It doesn't matter*
   [It doesn't do anything]

Çe n'est pas très important de le faire *It isn't very important to do it*
Ça n'a pas beaucoup d'importance *It doesn't have much importance*

Ça me fait plaisir *It gives me pleasure [It makes*
   me pleasure]

Ça me fait grand plaisir… *I am very pleased…*
…de vous voir *…to see you*
…de le faire pour vous *…to do it for you*
Ça me fera grand plaisir de vous voir *It will give me great pleasure to see you,*
   I am looking forward to seeing you

Je suis fatigué *I am tired*
Je suis épuisé *I am exhausted*
Je dois me reposer *I must rest [I must rest myself]*
Je vais me reposer *I am going to have a rest [rest myself]*

Il y a beaucoup de bruit *There is much noise*
Il y a trop de bruit *There is too much noise*
On fait trop de bruit *One is making too much noise*
Ça fait trop de bruit *It makes too much noise*
Ça me dérange *It disturbs me [It deranges me]*

Ça me dérange beaucoup	*It disturbs me very much*
Ça ne me dérange pas	*It doesn't disturb me*
Ça ne me dérange pas du tout	*It doesn't disturb me at all*
Ça m'ennuie	*It annoys me*
Ça ne m'ennuie pas	*It doesn't annoy me*

J'ai l'impression qu'... — *I have the impression that...*

...elle ne le veut pas	*...she doesn't want it*
...elle ne veut pas le faire	*...she doesn't want to do it*
Je veux le faire mais je ne le ferai pas aujourd'hui...	*I want to do it but I won't do it today...*
...parce que je suis trop occupé pour le faire aujourd'hui	*...because I am too busy to [in order to] do it today*

You can push the 'p' of trop *into* occupé

Il me semble qu'... — *It seems [to me] that...*

...elle n'a pas envie d'y aller	*...she doesn't feel like going there*
A mon avis...	*In my opinion...*
...je suis d'accord avec vous	*... I agree [I am in accord] with you*
C'est d'accord	*It's OK*
D'accord	*OK, agreed*

Ca m'intéresse beaucoup — *It interests me a great deal*

Ca m'intéresse énormément	*It interests me enormously*
Mais malheureusement ça ne m'intéresse pas du tout	*But unfortunately it doesn't interest me at all*

Je ne crois pas qu'... — *I don't think [believe] that...*

...il va être là cet après-midi	*...he is going to be there this afternoon*

…mais on verra	*…but we will see*
Je ne sais pas si je peux le faire mais on verra	*I don't know if I can do it but we will see*
Ce ne sera pas possible de le faire comme ça	*It won't be possible to do it this way*
Je ne le crois pas	*I don't think so, I don't believe it*
Je ne le pense pas	*I don't think so*
Êtes-vous sûr? / Vous êtes sûr? / Est-ce que vous êtes sûr?	*Are you sure?*
Bien sûr / Naturellement	*Of course*
Bien sûr je suis sûr	*Of course I'm sure*
Regardez!	*Look!*
C'est sur la table	*It's on the table*

Voulez-vous le mettre…	*Will you put it…*
…sous la table?	*…under the table?*
…par terre?	*…on the floor [terra, land]?*
C'est par terre	*It's on the floor*
Je vais le mettre par terre	*I'm going to put it on the floor*
Voulez-vous le mettre là par terre?	*Will you put it there on the floor?*
Nous devons y aller	*We have to / must go there*
C'est nécessaire d'y aller	
Il faut…	*One / We must…*
…y aller maintenant	*…go there now*
…y aller tout de suite	*…go there right away*

Je voudrais l'avoir tout de suite	*I would like to have it right away*
Il me faut l'avoir tout de suite	*I must have it straightaway*
Je dois l'avoir tout de suite	

Il ne faut pas…	*One / We must not…*
…l'acheter	*…buy it*
On ne doit pas l'acheter…	*We must not buy it…*
…parce que c'est trop cher	*…because it's too expensive*

Il me faut ce livre, c'est tout	*I need this book, that's all*
C'est tout ce que…	*That's all (that)…*
…je veux	*…I want*
…vous voulez	*…you want*
Oui, c'est tout ce qu'il me faut	*That's all I need [all that is necessary to me]*

Est-ce qu'il vous faut autre chose?	*Do you need anything else?*
Non merci	*No thank you*
Ça sera tout	*That will be all*

Voulez-vous me montrer?	*Will you show me?*
Voulez-vous me faire voir?	*Will you let me [make me] see?*
Je vais vous faire voir autre chose	*I am going to show you something else*

Je peux vous faire voir autre chose	*I can show you something else*
Voulez-vous me faire voir ce que vous avez?	*Will you show me what you have?*

Voulez-vous me faire savoir?	*Will you let me [make me] know?*
Je vous ferai savoir demain	*I will let you [make you] know tomorrow*

Je vais vous faire savoir demain	I am going to let you know tomorrow
Voulez-vous me faire savoir…	Will you let me know…
…à quelle heure ça sera prêt?	…at what time it will be ready?
…à quelle heure ça va être prêt?	…at what time it is going to be ready?

se renseigner — *to find out [to enquire oneself]*

enseigner	to teach
le guichet de renseignements	enquiries window
Je vais me renseigner	I'm going to find out
Voulez-vous vous renseigner?	Will you find out?
J'ai besoin d'un renseignement	I need [I have need of] information
Il me faut des renseignements	I need some information

Je dois me renseigner…	I must find out…
…et je vous ferai savoir demain	…and I will let you know tomorrow
…et je vais vous faire savoir demain	…and I am going to let you know tomorrow

pouvoir — *to be able to*

le pouvoir	the power
Il n'a pas le pouvoir de le faire	He does not have the power to do it
Il ne peut pas le faire	He cannot do it
Je ne peux pas le faire	I cannot do it
Je ne vais pas pouvoir le faire	I am not going to be able to do it
Je pourrai le faire	I will be able to do it
Je ne pourrai pas le faire	I will not be able to do it

In the future tense, pouvoir *contracts. Other verbs ending in –oir are similar in the future tense:* voir (je verrai) savoir (je saurai), devoir (je devrai)

Je ne pourrai pas le trouver ici	I won't be able to find it here

En avez-vous?	*Do you have any (of it)?*
Est-ce que vous en avez?	
Non, je n'en ai pas	*No, I don't have any (of it)*
Il y en a	*There is / are some (of it)*
Il y en a encore	*There is / are still some,*
	There is / are still some left
Je n'en ai plus	*I don't have any more (of it)*
Il n'y en a plus	*There is / are no more (of it)*
	(We're out of it)
Il n'y en a pas	*There isn't / aren't any (of it)*
Je regrette…	*I'm sorry…*
Je suis désolé…	
…mais il n'y en a plus	*…but there aren't any more of it*
Comment allez-vous?	*How are you? [How are you going?]*
Je vais bien merci. Et vous?	*I'm fine [going well]. And you?*
Ça va bien	*I'm / It's fine, I'm / It's all right*
Je me débrouille	*I get by, I manage, I am managing*
Je me débrouille en français	*I get by in French*
Je me débrouillerai	*I will manage, I will find a way*
	(to do something)
Je ne sais pas comment mais…	*I don't know how but…*
…je vais me débrouiller	*…I am going to manage*

You use de *after* demander, dire *and* decider *if they are followed by a full verb (infinitive)*

Je vais décider de…	*I am going to decide to…*
Je vais décider de le faire	*I am going to decide to do it*
Je ne peux pas décider de le faire	*I cannot decide to do it*

Je vais lui demander	*I'm going to ask him / her*
Je vais leur demander	*I'm going to ask them*
Je vais lui demander…	*I'm going to ask him / her…*
…s'il peut / si elle peut le faire	*…if he can / if she can do it*
…de venir avec nous	*…to come with us*
Je voudrais vous demander de…	*I would like to ask you…*
…venir avec nous	*…to come with us*
Voulez-vous lui dire d'…	*Will you tell him / her…*
…attendre?	*…to wait?*
Voulez-vous lui demander de m'appeler plus tard?	*Will you ask him / her to call me later?*
Je crois qu'il va décider de le faire	*I think that he will decide to do it*
Je suis décidé de le faire tout de suite	*I am decided / determined to do it immediately*
essayer	*to try, to try on*
Je voudrais…	*I would like…*
Je voudrais l'essayer	*I would like to try it on*
Puis-je…?	*May I?*
Puis-je le voir ?	*May I see it?*
Est-ce que je peux le voir?	*Can I see it ?*
Vous permettez?	*Is it all right? May I? [you permit?]*

You use de after essayer and oublier if a verb follows

Je vais essayer de…	*I am going to try…*
…le faire	*…to do it*
Je ne sais pas si je peux le faire…	*I don't know if I can do it…*
…mais je vais essayer de le faire	*…but I am going to try to do it*

Je ne vais pas oublier de… *I am not going to forget…*
…le faire *…to do it*
…vous dire *…to tell you*
…vous le donner *…to give it to you*
…le lui donner *…to give it to him / her*

When there are two 'l's, as in le lui *and* le leur, le *comes before the pronoun beginning with 'l'. When there is only one 'l', all other pronouns* (me, te, nous, vous) *come before* le

---

Je voudrais vous le donner *I would like to give it to you*
Je voudrais le lui donner *I would like to give it to him / her*
Je ne vais pas oublier de… *I am not going to forget…*
Je n'oublierai pas de… *I won't forget…*
…le lui donner *…to give it to him / her*

J'ai vraiment envie de le faire… *I really feel like doing it…*
…mais je ne sais pas si je peux *…but I don't know if I can do it*
  le faire
J'essayerai / Je vais essayer *I will / I am going to try to do it*
  de le faire

Elle voudrait essayer la robe *She would like to try on the dress*
Il voudrait l'essayer *He would like to try it on*

Est-ce que ça vaut la peine *Is it worth going there?*
  d'y aller?
Ça vaut la peine d'y aller?
Ça ne vaut pas la peine de le faire *It's not worth doing it*
On peut y aller maintenant *One / We can go there now*
  si vous voulez *if you want*

You can push the 't' of peut *into* y aller

Voulez-vous lui demander de m'attendre? *Will you ask him / her to wait for me?*

Voulez-vous lui dire de m'attendre? *Will you tell him / her to wait for me?*

Voulez-vous venir avec moi? *Will you come with me?*
  Do you want to come with me?

Oui, certainement. *Yes, certainly*
Je voudrais bien *I would like to*
Je veux bien *I want to*
D'accord, certainement *Agreed, certainly*
Volontiers *Gladly*
Vous êtes très gentil *You are very nice*
C'est très gentil de votre part *It's very nice of you*

D'accord? C'est d'accord? *OK? Is it OK?*
Ça vous va? *Does it agree with you?*
  [It goes with you?] Is it OK with you?

Ça vous convient? *Is it all right with you?*
  [It convenes with you?]

Ça me convient *It's all right with me*
Ça va bien *It's going well*
Ça ne me convient pas *It's not all right with me,*
  It's not convenient for me

J'aime ça *I like that*
Ça me plaît *It pleases me*
C'est une bonne idée *It's a good idea*
J'aime cette idée *I like that idea*
Ça c'est une bonne idée *That is a good idea*

Recording 2

J'aime…	*I like…*
J'aime beaucoup…	*I like very much…*
J'aime beaucoup voyager	*I like very much to travel*
	very much like travelling

passer le temps	*to spend time*
passer le weekend	*to spend the weekend*
Je crois que je vais passer	*I think [believe] that I am going to*
mes vacances	*spend my vacation*
…d'abord en France	*…first in France*
…et puis / plus tard en Italie	*…and then / later in Italy*

Je pense…	*I plan on…*

penser *means 'to think' and also 'to plan'*

Je pense partir bientôt	*I plan on leaving [think to leave] soon*
Quand pensez-vous partir?	*When do you plan on leaving*
	[think to leave]?
Combien de temps pensez-vous rester?	*How long do you plan on staying?*
Je pense partir lundi	*I plan on leaving Monday*
Je pense partir lundi prochain	*I plan on leaving next Monday*

DAYS OF THE WEEK

Most of the days of the week are named after Latin and Greek gods and the planets:

lundi [moon's day, from lune,	*Monday*
'moon' + dies, 'day' in Latin]	
mardi [mars' day]	*Tuesday*

mardi prochain, mardi matin	*next Tuesday, Tuesday morning*
mercredi *[mercury's day]*	*Wednesday*
mercredi prochain, mercredi soir	*next Wednesday, Wednesday evening*
jeudi *[Jove's day]*	*Thursday*
vendredi *[venus' day]*	*Friday*
samedi *[Sabbath day]*	*Saturday*
dimanche *[the Lord's day, from dominicus, 'of a lord' in Latin]*	*Sunday*
dimanche matin	*Sunday morning*

MONTHS OF THE YEAR

janvier	*January*
en janvier, au mois de janvier	*in January, in the month of January*
le mois prochain	*the next month, next month*
dans un mois	*in a month*
février, au mois de février	*February, in the month of February*
mars, avril, mai, juin, juillet, août, septembre, octobre, novembre, décembre	*March, April, May, June, July, August, September, October, November, December*
Je pense…	*I plan on…*
…passer quelques semaines en France	*…spending a few weeks in France*
J'espère…	*I expect to, I hope to…*
…passer quelques semaines en France	*…spend a few weeks in France*
J'ai l'intention de…	*I intend to…*
…passer quelques semaines en France	*…spend a few weeks in France*
J'espère passer plusieurs semaines en France	*I expect/hope to spend several weeks in France*

J'ai l'intention de partir la semaine prochaine	*I intend to leave next week*
Je vous verrai / je vais vous voir…	*I will see you / I'm going to see you…*
…dans huit jours	*…in a week*
il y a huit jours	*eight days ago*

Je vais partir… *I am going to leave…*

…dans deux semaines / dans quinze jours	*…in two weeks / in a fortnight*
Je vous verrai / je vais vous voir…	*I am going to / I will see…*
…dans quinze jours	*…in two weeks*
Nous allons arriver dans quinze jours	*We will arrive in two weeks*

ASKING FOR DIRECTIONS

If you stop a policeman to ask for directions you will say Pardon Monsieur. *Simply say* Pour aller à…(to go to…), *the place you want to go to and* s'il vous plaît? *(please?). Using a questioning tone of voice you can even say just the name of the place and* s'il vous plaît?

Pardon Monsieur/Madame/ Mademoiselle …	*Excuse me…*
…pour aller à la Place de l'Opéra s'il vous plaît?	*…(can you tell me) the way to*
…la Place de l'Opéra s'il vous plaît?	*Place de l'Opéra please?*
…pour aller à Lyon s'il vous plaît ?	*…(can you tell me) the way to Lyon / the road for Lyon?*

Traversez la rue… *Cross the street …*
…puis vous continuez tout droit *… then you continue / keep going straight ahead*

…vous tournez à gauche	*…turn left*
…vous tournez à droite	*…turn right*

…à la troisième rue vous tournez à droite	…at the third street you turn right
C'est à votre droite	It is on the right side / to your right
C'est à votre gauche	It is on the left side / to your left

Note the difference between tout droit *'straight ahead' and* à droite *'on the right' (the 't' is sounded here).*

C'est en face	It is right in front
C'est de ce côté	It is on this side
C'est de l'autre côté	It is on the other side
Je vous remercie beaucoup	I thank you very much
Merci mille fois	Thanks a thousand times / many times

C'est par ici	It is this way
Vous pouvez le trouver…	You can find it…
…par ici	…this way
…par là	…that way
Vous allez le trouver par là	You will find it that way
C'est par là	It is that way
C'est au coin	It is at the corner
C'est au coin de la rue	It is on the corner of the road
Ce n'est pas loin d'ici, c'est au coin de la rue	It is not far from here, it is on the corner of the street
C'est au bout de la rue	It is at the end of the street
C'est tout de suite là au bout de la rue	It is right there at the end of the street
C'est là, C'est là-bas	It is there, It is over there [there down]
Vous pouvez le trouver là-bas	You can find it over there

aussi…que *means 'as…as';* aussi *by itself means 'also';* non plus *means 'neither'*

29

Voulez-vous lui demander…	*Will you ask him…*
…de me l'envoyer?	*…to send it to me?*
…aussi vite que possible?	*…as quickly as possible?*

Je le ferai aussi	*I will also do it*
Ça me plaît aussi	*It pleases me also, I like it also*
Je ne le veux pas	*I don't want it*
Je ne le veux plus	*I don't want it any more*
Moi non plus	*Me neither*

Pouvez-vous le faire aussitôt que possible?	*Can you do it as soon as possible?*
Pouvez-vous être ici aussi vite que possible?	*Can you be here as quickly as possible?*
Je vais l'arranger pour vous aussi vite que possible	*I am going to arrange it for you as quickly as possible*

Je vous prie de…	*I beg you to…*
…le faire	*…do it*
…l'arranger pour moi	*…arrange it for me*
Voulez-vous…	*Will you…*
…le faire s'il vous plaît?	*…do it please?*
…l'arranger pour moi s'il vous plaît?	*…arrange it for me please?*
Voulez-vous venir avec moi…	*Will you come with me…*
…s'il vous plaît?	*…please?*
…je vous prie ?	*…I beg you?*

Je vous prie (*from* prier, *'to beg'*) is a more emphatic form of 'please'

C'est…	*It is…*
…terrible	*…terrible*
…horrible	*…horrible*
…affreux	*…awful*

Je vais me renseigner	*I am going to find out [inform myself]*
Je dois me renseigner	*I must find out*
Je viens de me renseigner	*I have just found out*
	[I come from finding out]

Voulez-vous essayer de… *Will you try to…*
…l'obtenir pour moi? *…get it for me?*
Je vais essayer de… *I am going to try to…*
…l'obtenir pour vous *…get it for you*
…de le faire *…to do it*

Je vais prendre l'avion… *I am going to take the plane…*
…pour aller à Londres *…to go [in order to go] to London*

Ça marche *It works, it functions [it marches]*
Ça marche bien comme ça *It works well like that*
Ça ne marche pas *It doesn't work*
Ça ne marche pas bien *It doesn't work well*

Use faire for 'to have something done'

Je veux faire laver mes chemises *I want to get / have my shirts washed*
Voulez-vous… *Will you…*
…faire nettoyer mon costume? *… have my suit cleaned [made neat]?*
…faire nettoyer la robe? *…have the dress cleaned?*
…le faire nettoyer? *…have it cleaned ?*
…le faire réparer? *…have it repaired?*
…le faire laver? *…have it washed?*
…le faire repasser? *…have it ironed?*
…le faire attendre? *…have him wait, make him wait?*
…le faire monter (dans ma chambre)? *…have him come up to my room?*
…faire descendre mes valises? *…have my luggage taken down?*

31

…le faire monter?	*…have it taken up?*
…faire monter mon petit-déjeuner?	*…have my breakfast brought up?*
…me faire réveiller demain matin à huit heures?	*…have me awakened / woken up tomorrow morning at eight o'clock?*
…me faire savoir ?	*…let me know*

> monter *means 'to go up', 'to come up', 'to bring up', 'to take up', 'to carry up' etc;* descendre *means 'to go down', 'to bring down', 'to take down', 'to carry down'*

Je vous ferai savoir	*I will let you know*
Je vais vous faire savoir	*I am going to let you know*
Voulez-vous le faire changer?	*Will you have it changed?*

Pouvez-vous me montrer autre chose?	*Can you show me something else?*
Pouvez-vous me faire voir autre chose?	*" " " [Can you make me see…?]*
Je vais le faire faire	*I am going to have it done [to make it do]*
Voulez-vous le faire faire pour moi?	*Will you have it done / made for me?*
Voulez-vous faire venir un docteur?	*Will you get [make come] a doctor?*
Voulez-vous faire venir un taxi?	*Will you get a taxi?*
Voulez-vous appeler un taxi?	*Will you call a taxi?*
Voulez-vous passer le sucre?	*Will you pass the sugar?*

Puis-je…?	*May I…?*
Puis-je le voir?	*May I see it?*

> *If you are reaching out for something, you will say* Vous permettez? *[You permit?] 'May I?' Or, if someone says this to you, you will reply* Je vous prie *[I beg you] or* Je vous en prie *[I beg you of it] 'Please do'.*

Voulez-vous le réparer pour moi?	*Will you repair it for me?*
Voulez-vous le faire réparer pour moi?	*Will you have it repaired for me?*

Pardon?	*Pardon?, Pardon me?, Excuse me?* *(when you want someone to repeat something)*
Comment?	*" " " " [How ?]*
Vous dites?	*Will you repeat it, please?* *[You are saying?]*
Je voudrais le dire…	*I would like to say it…*
…mais je ne sais pas comment l'exprimer en français	*…but I don't know how to express it in French*
Je voudrais savoir comment m'exprimer mieux en français	*I would like to know how to express myself better in French*
Comment ça se dit en français?	*How does one say it in French? How do you say it…? [How does it say itself?]*
Je voudrais savoir comment ça se dit en français	*I would like to know how it is being said in French*
Voulez-vous me dire / Pourriez-vous me dire comment ça se dit en français ?	*Will you / Could you tell me how one says it in French?*
Comment ça s'écrit en français?	*How do you spell it in French? [How does it write itself?]*
Je suis certain / sûr qu'il va avoir beaucoup de difficultés	*I am certain / sure that he is going to have a lot of trouble*

ENGLISH WORDS ENDING IN '–TY'
All English words ending in '–ty' end in –té in French: liberty liberté,
opportunity opportunité, *facility* facilité, *difficulty* difficulté. *Similarly,
English words ending in '–em' end in –ème in French: problem*
problème, *system* système

On va avoir beaucoup de problèmes	*One is going to have many problems*
vouloir dire	*to mean*
Vous voulez dire…	*You mean… [You want to say…]*
Je veux dire…	*I mean…*
Ce n'est pas ce que je veux dire	*That's not what I mean*
Qu'est-ce que vous voulez dire?	*What do you mean?*
	[What do you want to say?]
Je ne comprends pas ce que vous voulez dire	*I don't understand what you mean*
Ça veut dire…	*It means…*
Voulez-vous expliquer ce que vous voulez dire?	*Will you explain what you mean?*
Pouvez-vous expliquer ce que ça veut dire?	*Can you explain what that means?*
Qu'est-ce que ça veut dire?	*What does it mean?*
Je ne comprends pas ce que ça veut dire	*I don't understand what it means*
Voulez-vous prendre un verre?	*Do you want a drink? [Do you want to take a glass?]*
Voulez-vous prendre un verre avec moi?	*Will you have a drink with me?*
Comme vous voulez	*As you like*
Si vous voulez	*If you like, If you want*
Ça m'est égal	*I don't care [It is equal to me]*
Ça ne vaut pas la peine d'insister	*It's not worth insisting*
Ce n'est pas la peine d'insister	*Why insist? Don't bother insisting*
C'est évident	*It is evident*

possible, possiblement	*possible, possibly*
confortable, confortablement	*comfortable, comfortably*
évident, évidemment	*evidently*
récent, récemment	*recent, recently*
constant, constamment	*constant, constantly*
Il le fait constamment	*He is doing it constantly*
Il fait la même chose constamment	*He is doing the same thing constantly*
pas très fréquemment	*not very frequently*
fréquenter	*to frequent, to go often to*
J'aime fréquenter ce restaurant	*I like to frequent this restaurant*

Ça ne fait rien	*It doesn't matter*
	[It doesn't do anything]
Ça m'est égal	*It is all the same to me, I don't care*
Vraiment?	*Really, Is that so? [Truly?]*
Tant mieux	*So much the better*
C'est tant mieux comme ça	*It's much better that way*
Tant pis	*Too bad, So much the worse, So what?*
Il n'y a pas de problèmes	*There are no problems*
Je suis fâché	*I am angry*

soirée, journée, matinée	
Merci pour cette agréable soirée	*Thank you for that lovely evening*
donner une soirée	*to give an evening party*

C'est / C'était une soirée agréable	*It is / was a pleasant [agreeable] evening*
passer une journée	*to spend a (whole) day*
passer une matinée	*to spend a (whole) morning*

ensemble — *together*

Si vous voulez nous pouvons / on peut aller au cinéma ensemble	*If you want, we can go to the movies together*
On peut y aller en voiture	*We can go there by car*

C'est ridicule	*It is ridiculous*
C'est dommage	*It is too bad*
Je vous remercie	*I thank you*

Il me semble que… — *It seems to me that…*

…tout va bien — *…everything is all right [is going well]*

au moins — *at least [at less]*

Je voudrais y aller…	*I would like to go there…*
…au moins je verrai ce que c'est	*…at least I will see what it is*

spécialement — *specially*

C'est (très) spécial	*It is very special*
la spécialité	*the speciality*
Quelle spécialité avez-vous?	*What speciality do you have?*
Quelle est la spécialité de la maison?	*What is the speciality of the house?*
Spécialement si vous pouvez me dire ce que vous pensez	*Especially if you can tell me what you think*
Surtout si vous pouvez me dire…	*Above all / Mainly if you can tell me…*

réfléchir — *to reflect, to think about*

Je vais réfléchir	*I am going to think about it*
Laissez-moi réfléchir	*Let me think about it*

Je vais vous faire savoir dans huit jours	*I am going to let you know in a week*
Je vous ferai savoir…	*I will let you know…*
Ça va très bien	*It is going very well*
Ca va beaucoup mieux	*It is going much better*

sentir — *to feel*

Je le sens	*I feel it*
Je me sens bien	*I feel fine [feel myself]*
Je me sens mieux	*I feel better*
Je me sens beaucoup mieux aujourd'hui	*I feel much better today*
Je me sens beaucoup mieux quand je suis seul	*I feel much better when I am alone*
Je travaille beaucoup mieux quand je suis seul	*I work much better when I am alone*

Je n'ai besoin de rien	*I don't need / have need of anything*
Je n'en ai pas besoin	*I don't need / have need of it*
J'ai besoin de ça	*I need / have need of that*
J'en ai besoin	*I need / have need of it*

Il y a trop de monde ici	*There are too many people here*
Tout le monde est ici	*Everybody is here*
Tout le monde va être ici	*Everybody is going to be here*
Tout le monde va être là ce soir	*Everybody is going to be there tonight*
Il y a beaucoup de monde	*There are many people*
Je ne veux pas rester ici…	*I don't want to stay here…*
…parce qu'il y a trop de monde ici	*… because there are too many people here*
…aussi il fait très chaud ici	*…also it is very warm here*

Il n'y a pas de climatisation ici	*There is no air-conditioning here*
Ce n'est pas climatisé	*It is not air-conditioned*
Je ne peux pas supporter la chaleur	*I cannot stand the heat*

To say 'It is…' when you are talking about the weather, use Il fait… *[it makes…], not* C'est…

Il fait…	*It is…*
…chaud	…*warm, hot*
…beau	…*fine, beautiful weather*
…beau temps	… « « « «
…froid	…*cold*

avoir froid / chaud	*to be [to have] cold / warm*
J'ai chaud	*I am [have] warm*
Avez-vous froid?	*Are you cold?*

Note: If you say Êtes-vous froid? *this means 'Are you a cold person?'*

Nous avons chaud ici	*We are warm here*
Il fait chaud ici	*It is warm here*
J'ai froid…	*I am cold…*
…parce qu'il fait froid ici	…*because it is cold here*

avoir faim / soif	*to be hungry / thirsty*
J'ai faim	*I am hungry [I have hunger / famine]*
Je n'ai pas faim	*I am not hungry*
Je voudrais manger quelque chose…	*I would like to eat something…*
…parce que j'ai faim	…*because I am hungry*
J'ai soif	*I am thirsty*
Je voudrais boire quelque chose…	*I would like to drink something…*
…parce que j'ai soif	…*because I am thirsty*
Qu'est-ce que vous voulez boire?	*What do you want to drink?*

prendre   *to take, to have (food or drink)*
Qu'est-ce que vous voulez prendre?   *What would you like to have
                                                      (to eat or drink)?*

If you want to say 'have' referring to food or drink, never use avoir.
Instead use prendre *meaning 'to take [intake]'*

Je vais prendre une tasse de café   *I'm going to have [take]
                                                          a cup of coffee*
Je vais prendre mon petit-déjeuner   *I am going to have my breakfast*
Voulez-vous prendre le petit-déjeuner *Will you have breakfast with me?*
   avec moi?
À quelle heure voulez-vous prendre   *At what time do you want to have
   le petit-déjeuner demain matin?   breakfast tomorrow morning?*

Je vais faire des achats   *I am going shopping
                                                          [to do purchases]*

moi-même   *myself*
Je pense/crois que je peux le faire   *I think I can do it myself*
   moi-même
Je vais essayer de le faire moi-même   *I am going to try to do it myself*
quand même   *anyway, even so*
Je vais le faire quand même   *I am going to do it anyway*
Je le ferai quand même   *I will do it anyway*
même si…   *even if…*
Même si vous me dites que je ne   *Even if you tell me that I cannot
   peux pas le faire…   do it…*
…je vais essayer de le faire   *…I am going to try to do it anyway*
   quand même

Je vais le faire lentement	*I am going to do it slowly*
Ça ne va pas très bien	*It is not going very well*
Ça va mal	*It is going badly*
Ça m'étonne	*It astonishes me, surprises me*
Je suis surpris	*I am surprised*
Il est surpris	*He is surprised*
Il est bien surpris	*He is quite surprised*

bien *before an adjective means 'quite'*

Elle est surprise	*She is surprised*
Êtes-vous surpris / surprise?	*Are you surprised?*

If you are talking about a woman, add 'e' to surpris *to make it feminine*

Ça ne m'étonne pas	*It doesn't surprise me*
C'est...	*It is...*
...magnifique	*...magnificent*
...superbe	*...superb*
...formidable	*...great*
...fantastique	*...fantastic, tremendous*
mauvais / mal	*bad / badly*
C'est très mauvais	*It is very bad*
Ça ne me plaît pas parce que c'est très mauvais	*I don't like it because it is very bad*
Il le fait mal	*He is doing it badly*
Ça va mal	*It is going badly*
Ça ne va pas mal aujourd'hui	*It is not going badly today*
Au contraire, ça va très bien	*On the contrary, it is going very well*

C'est très léger — *It is very light*
C'est très lourd — *It is very heavy*
C'est trop lourd — *It is too heavy*

lever / se lever — *to lift / to get up*
Je le lève — *I am lifting it up*
Je me lève — *I am getting up [lifting myself up]*
Je vais me lever — *I am going to get up*
Je vais me lever tôt — *I am going to get up early*
Je vais me lever plus tôt — *I am going to get up earlier*
C'est trop tôt — *It is too early*
Je vais me lever de bonne heure demain matin — *I am going to get up early [of good hour] tomorrow morning*

C'est très lourd — *It is very heavy*
Je ne peux pas le lever… — *I cannot lift it up…*
…parce que c'est trop lourd — *…because it is too heavy*
C'est plein — *It is full*
C'est trop plein — *It is too full*

remplir — *to fill up / to fill in (a form)*
Voulez-vous remplir la fiche? — *Will you fill in the form?*
C'est très vide — *It is very empty [void]*
C'est trop vide — *It is too empty*
vider — *to empty*
Je vais le vider — *I am going to empty it*
Voulez-vous remplir le verre? — *Will you fill up the glass?*
Voulez-vous remplir la bouteille? — *Will you fill up the bottle?*

Ce n'est pas propre — *It is not clean*
Voulez-vous le nettoyer? — *Will you clean it up?*
C'est très sale — *It is very dirty*
C'est trop sale — *It is too dirty*

41

répondre	*to answer [respond]*
donner une réponse	*to give an answer*
Voulez-vous me donner une réponse?	*Will you give me an answer?*
J'attends votre réponse	*I am waiting for your answer*
Voulez-vous me répondre?	*Will you answer me?*
C'est parfait	*It is perfect*
C'est vraiment parfait	*It is really perfect*
Où voulez-vous le mettre?	*Where do you want to put it?*
Je voudrais savoir où c'est	*I would like to know where it is?*
Ça se trouve…	*It is [finds itself]…*
Je voudrais savoir où ça se trouve	*I would like to know where it is located*
Je voudrais savoir où est / se trouve le restaurant	*I would like to know where is the restaurant*
Le restaurant est / se trouve près d'ici	*The restaurant is near here*
Le restaurant se trouve tout près d'ici	*The restaurant is quite near here*
Vous pouvez aller à pied	*You can walk there*
Ce n'est pas loin	*It is not far*
n'importe où	*anywhere, anyplace, no matter where*
Vous pouvez l'avoir n'importe où	*You can get it anywhere*
Vous pouvez le trouver n'importe où	*You can find it anyplace*
n'importe qui	*anybody*
N'importe qui peut vous dire	*Anybody can tell you*
n'importe quand	*any time, no matter when*
Vous pouvez venir n'importe quand	*You can come any time*
à n'importe quelle heure	*at any time*
Vous pouvez venir à n'importe quelle heure	*You can come at any time*

Vous pouvez le faire à n'importe quelle heure / n'importe quand	*You can do it at any time / no matter when*
n'importe comment	*anyhow, no matter how*

Je le cherche **partout…**	*I am looking for it everywhere…*
…mais vous pouvez le trouver n'importe où	*…but you can find it anyplace*

sans	*without*
Je ne peux pas le faire sans vous	*I can't do it without you*
sans souci	*without worries*
sans…	*without…*
…me dire	*…telling me*
…le trouver	*…finding it*
…partir	*…leaving*
…dire un mot	*…saying a word*
Il va partir sans dire un mot	*He is going to leave without saying a word*

For verbs in English which end in '-ing' (e.g. doing, making…) and which follow a preposition (e.g. sans), you use the whole verb (infinitive) in French

Ç'est assez	*It is enough*
Ça suffit	*It / That is enough [It suffices]*
Ça suffit pour aujourd'hui	*It is enough for today*
C'est assez comme ça	*It is enough like that*

Bon voyage!	*Good trip!*
Bonne chance!	*Good luck!*
souhaiter	*to wish*
Je vous souhaite bonne chance	*I wish you good luck*
À vos souhaits	*to your wishes (said after sneezing)*
À bientôt	*until soon*

The Michel Thomas Language Range

8-hour Language Courses*

These all-audio courses provide an accelerated method for learning that is truly revolutionary. In just a few hours, anyone can gain a functional working knowledge of a language, without books, note-taking or conscious memorising.

The first 2 hours of the 8-hour course are also available separately – see order form opposite for details.

Language Builders

The perfect follow-on to the 8-hour course. In 2 hours, you will increase your word power and gain extra confidence in your pronunciation. With a full listing of all the crucial words and phrases, you will able to improve your spelling, reading and writing too.

If you would like to find out more, please get in touch with us

For general enquiries:
Call: 020 7873 6261   Fax: 020 7873 6299
Email: michelthomas-enquiries@hodder.co.uk

To place an order, please fill in the order form on the next page and send it to the FREEPOST address listed, or:
Call: 01235 400414   Fax: 01235 400454
Email: orders@bookpoint.co.uk

You can write to us at: Hodder & Stoughton Educational, 338 Euston Road, London NW1 3BH

Visit our website at: www.madaboutbooks.com

MICHEL THOMAS ORDER FORM

Please complete and send back to us at the FREEPOST address listed below.

2-hour course CD £14.99			**2-hour course cassette £14.99**		
French	ISBN 0 340 78064 9	☐	French	ISBN 0 340 77550 5	☐
German	ISBN 0 340 78066 5	☐	German	ISBN 0 340 77551 3	☐
Italian	ISBN 0 340 78070 3	☐	Italian	ISBN 0 340 77553 X	☐
Spanish	ISBN 0 340 78068 1	☐	Spanish	ISBN 0 340 77552 1	☐

8-hour course CD £70			**8-hour course cassette £70**		
French	ISBN 0 340 78063 0	☐	French	ISBN 0 340 77554 8	☐
German	ISBN 0 340 78065 7	☐	German	ISBN 0 340 77555 6	☐
Italian	ISBN 0 340 78069 X	☐	Italian	ISBN 0 340 77557 2	☐
Spanish	ISBN 0 340 78067 3	☐	Spanish	ISBN 0 340 77556 4	☐

Language Builder CD £20			**Language Builder Cassette £20**		
French	ISBN 0 340 78969 7	☐	French	ISBN 0 340 78968 9	☐
German	ISBN 0 340 78973 5	☐	German	ISBN 0 340 78972 7	☐
Italian	ISBN 0 340 78975 1	☐	Italian	ISBN 0 340 78974 3	☐
Spanish	ISBN 0 340 78971 9	☐	Spanish	ISBN 0 340 78970 0	☐

Title_____ Initials _____ Surname _____

Delivery Address _____

_____

_____ Postcode _____

Telephone _____

Methods of payment: Cash ☐ Cheque ☐ Credit Card ☐ Debit Card ☐

Please make cheques payable to Bookpoint Ltd

Card Number ☐ ☐ ☐ ☐ ☐ ☐ ☐ ☐ ☐ ☐ ☐ ☐ ☐ ☐ ☐ ☐

Expiry Details ☐ ☐ / ☐ ☐ Issue Number (Switch & Delta only) ☐

For orders under £20 please add £2.00 for p&p

Signature _____ **Total £** _____

Cardholder's Address (if different from above) _____

_____

Please send your completed order form to: **Michel Thomas Language Courses, Hodder & Stoughton Educational, FREEPOST NW6148, 338 Euston Road, London NW1 3YS**